I0814235

DISCOVERING THE UNITED STATES

Ohio

BY LIZ SONNEBORN

An Imprint of Abdo Publishing
abdobooks.com

abdobooks.com

Printed in China.
052024
092024

Cover Photo: Christian Hinkle/Shutterstock Images
Interior Photos: R. Scott James/Alamy, 4–5; Shutterstock Images, 7, 8 (bottom right), 18, 28 (bottom left); Bonnie Taylor Barry/Shutterstock Images, 8 (top left); Peter Turner Photography/Shutterstock Images, 8 (top right); Lama Saoudi/Shutterstock Images, 8 (bottom left); Sara Winter/Shutterstock Images, 10; Steeve-X-Art/Alamy, 12–13; Jason Miller/Getty Images Sport/Getty Images, 15; Robin Alam/Icon Sportswire/AP Images, 16; Sean Pavone/Shutterstock Images, 20–21, 22, 28 (top right); Jim West/Alamy, 25; Wanderlust Photo/Shutterstock Images, 26; Red Line Editorial, 28 (top left), 29; Joseph Hendrickson/Shutterstock Images, 28 (bottom right)

Editor: Marley Richmond
Series Designer: Katharine Hale

Library of Congress Control Number: 2023949364

Publisher's Cataloging-in-Publication Data

Names: Sonneborn, Liz, author.
Title: Ohio / by Liz Sonneborn
Description: Minneapolis, Minnesota: Abdo Publishing, 2025 | Series: Discovering the United States | Includes online resources and index.
Identifiers: ISBN 9781098294052 (lib. bdg.) | ISBN 9798384913320 (ebook)
Subjects: LCSH: U.S. states--Juvenile literature. | Ohio--History--Juvenile literature. | Midwest States--Juvenile literature. | Physical geography--United States--Juvenile literature.
Classification: DDC 973--dc23

All population data taken from:
"Estimates of Population by Sex, Race, and Hispanic Origin: April 1, 2020 to July 1, 2022." *US Census Bureau, Population Division*, June 2023, census.gov.

CONTENTS

A mural in Newark, Ohio, shows a boat on the Ohio and Erie Canal.

Building Ohio

On July 3, 1827, Joe Snyder gathered his 14 children. He told them they were setting out on a journey to see something amazing. They were going to see the Ohio and Erie **Canal**. The Snyders left from Green, Ohio.

They walked 9.5 miles (15.3 km) through the countryside.

After several hours, the Snyders reached the town of Akron. There, they spied a huge human-made ditch. It was filled with water. The ditch was the first section of the Ohio and Erie Canal. The canal would later connect the Ohio River to Lake Erie. The Snyders excitedly watched the first boat travel up the canal.

Before the canal was built, Ohio was a poor state. Farmers could not earn enough money. They had extra crops to sell, and people in cities to the east wanted to buy them. But it was too expensive to move crops across land. The canal allowed farmers to ship goods cheaply. New towns grew along the canal.

Goods are no longer shipped along the Ohio and Erie Canal. But people can still walk or bike along the canal's route on the Towpath Trail.

Ohio Facts

DATE OF STATEHOOD
March 1, 1803

CAPITAL
Columbus

POPULATION
11,756,058

AREA
44,826 square miles
(116,099 sq km)

STATE BIRD

Cardinal

STATE TREE

Ohio buckeye

STATE FLOWER

Red carnation

STATE INSECT

Ladybug

Each US state has a different population, size, and capital city. States also have state symbols.

More people **settled** in Ohio. It soon became a wealthy state with a large population. Nearly 200 years later, Ohio is still thriving.

Ohio Today

Ohio is in the Midwest region of the United States. Ohio shares a border with five states. Michigan borders Ohio to the northwest. Pennsylvania is to the east. West Virginia is to the southeast. Kentucky borders the state to the south, and Indiana is to the west.

The Animals of Ohio

Ohio is home to many animals. Large animals there include black bears and deer. Smaller mammals such as rabbits, squirrels, and raccoons are plentiful. The state's rivers are filled with pike, bass, perch, and catfish. Ducks are found in Lake Erie's marshes. Other birds include turkeys, partridges, and pheasants.

Marblehead Lighthouse stands along the coast of Lake Erie in Marblehead, Ohio.

Ohio's climate has four seasons. Summers are hot and **humid**. Winters are cold and often snowy.

Eastern Ohio has rolling hills and deep valleys. Western Ohio has low-lying plains.

To the north, sandy beaches run along the shore of Lake Erie. Lake Erie is one of five Great Lakes in North America.

Ohio has many bodies of water. The state has about 2,500 lakes. Ohio's rivers run more than 44,000 miles (70,800 km) total. The longest is the Ohio River. It forms Ohio's southern and southeastern border.

Explore Online

Visit the website below. What new information did you learn about the Ohio River?

Ohio River

abdocorelibrary.com/discovering-ohio

Tecumseh was a Shawnee leader born in Ohio. He fought to protect Shawnee land from white settlers.

CHAPTER 2

The People of Ohio

The first people who lived in Ohio were American Indians. The Adena people lived there about 2,800 years ago. Later American Indian peoples included the Shawnee, Delaware, and Wyandot.

Today, most Ohioans are white. Their **ancestors** were from European countries including England, Germany, and Poland. Many Black people also live in Ohio. They make up 13 percent of the population. About 4 percent of Ohioans are Hispanic or Latino. About 3 percent are Asian. Less than 1 percent are American Indian.

The Amish

Ohio has a large Amish population. The Amish are a religious group. Amish people avoid using modern technology. They travel in horse-drawn carriages and rarely use telephones or electricity. Four million tourists visit Ohio's Amish country each year. Visitors enjoy meals and crafts made by the Amish.

LeBron James played for the Cleveland Cavaliers from 2003 to 2010 and from 2014 to 2018.

Ohio has a large population. It is the seventh most **populated** US state. About 12 million people live there.

Some famous people come from Ohio. Basketball player LeBron James was born there. So was astronaut Neil Armstrong.

Ohio State University's football team is called the Buckeyes. Their mascot is Brutus Buckeye.

Culture

Many Ohioans love sports. Fans cheer on the Ohio State University football team. Ohioans also follow professional football teams, such as the Cincinnati Bengals and the Cleveland Browns. Baseball fans especially love the Cincinnati Reds.

Ohioans also enjoy many interesting foods. Cincinnati chili is a favorite. This dish is chili served over spaghetti noodles. Buckeyes are a tasty snack. They are peanut butter balls dipped in chocolate. They look like nuts from the buckeye tree. This tree gave Ohio its nickname, which is the Buckeye State.

Industry

Farming was once Ohio's most important industry. Ohio still makes good use of its farmland. But fewer people work on farms now than they once did.

Ohio is the only US state that does not have a rectangular flag.

Ohio's land has many **natural resources**. The state is a major **manufacturing** center. Factory workers make cars, machinery, chemicals, and more.

Most Ohio workers now hold service jobs. These include jobs in health care and the government. Other Ohioans work in stores, banks, or schools.

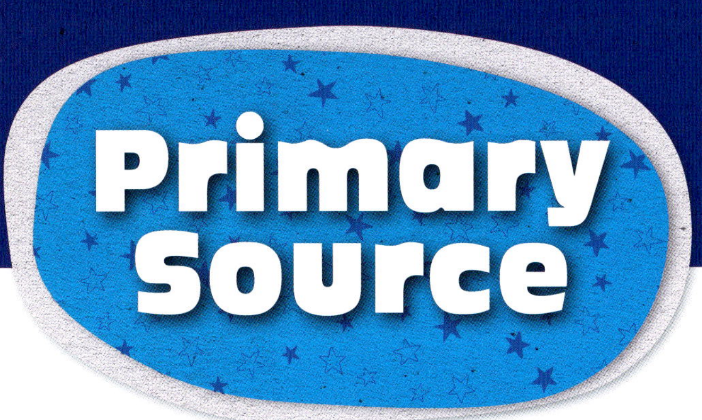

Ohioans are known for being friendly. Writer John Steinbeck described meeting Ohioans in his book *Travels with Charley*. He wrote:

> Almost on crossing the Ohio line it seemed to me that people were more open and more outgoing. . . . [The] earth was generous and outgoing here in the heartland, and perhaps the people took a cue from it.

Source: John Steinbeck. *Travels with Charley: In Search of America.* Penguin, 1997, p. 84.

What's the Big Idea?

Read the primary source carefully. What is its main idea? How does the author support this idea? Explain his idea in a few sentences.

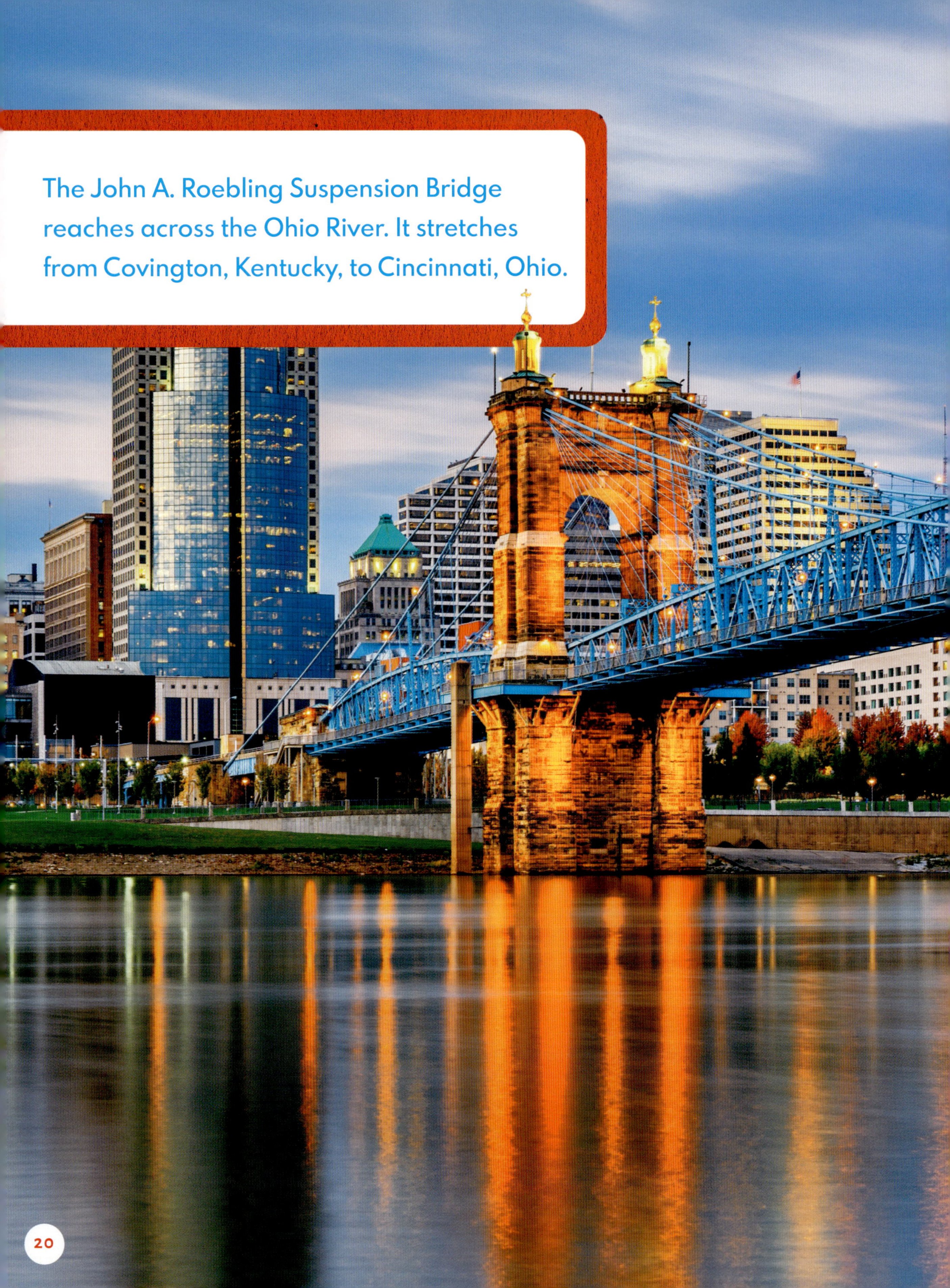

The John A. Roebling Suspension Bridge reaches across the Ohio River. It stretches from Covington, Kentucky, to Cincinnati, Ohio.

CHAPTER 3

Places in Ohio

Ohio is full of beautiful countryside. But most Ohioans live in or near cities. About half the population lives in Ohio's three biggest cities. They are Columbus, Cleveland, and Cincinnati.

Cleveland, Ohio, is known as the birthplace of rock and roll.

The largest city is Columbus. It is Ohio's capital. Columbus is in the middle of the state. Cleveland is in northeastern Ohio. It lies on the shore of Lake Erie. Cincinnati is in southwestern Ohio. It is on the Ohio River. Other major cities in Ohio include Toledo, Akron, and Dayton.

Landmarks

Ohio has many attractions. One is the Rock and Roll Hall of Fame. It is in Cleveland. Its museum displays rock stars' instruments and outfits.

Columbus has many more museums and landmarks. It is particularly known for Ohio Stadium. The stadium is called the Horseshoe because of its shape. The Ohio State Buckeyes play there. Columbus also has a popular zoo. It is home to 10,000 animals. They include elephants, giraffes, and lions. The show *Secrets of the Zoo* follows the animals there.

Toledo is sometimes called Glass City. It was once a glassmaking center. The Toledo Museum of Art is a famous attraction. Visitors can see many glass objects there.

The National Underground Railroad Freedom Center is in Cincinnati. This museum tells the story of enslaved people who sought freedom in the 1800s. Many of these people became free when they escaped into Ohio.

Cedar Point is an amusement park near Sandusky. It features 18 roller coasters and a water park. There is a popular beach close by.

The Soap Box Derby

Every year, Akron hosts the Soap Box Derby. The derby is a car race. The drivers are between seven and 20 years old. They build their own cars. Instead of using motors, these cars are powered by gravity. Riders drive them down a hill.

Visitors to the National Underground Railroad Freedom Center can see artwork exploring the family history of formerly enslaved people.

Brandywine Falls flows through Cuyahoga Valley National Park.

The Great Outdoors

Outdoor lovers in Ohio visit Cuyahoga Valley National Park. Visitors can walk the Towpath Trail. It traces the route of the Ohio and Erie Canal.

The Newark Earthworks also shows Ohio's history. This park is near the cities of Heath and Newark. It includes great mounds of earth. American Indian peoples made these earth mounds about 2,000 years ago. They were sacred places used for ceremonies.

Everywhere in Ohio, there are exciting things to see. Many landmarks celebrate the Buckeye State's past and show the bright future ahead.

Further Evidence

Look at the website below. Does it give any new evidence to support Chapter Three?

Columbus Zoo Animals

abdocorelibrary.com/discovering-ohio

State Map

KEY

Capital

Park

City or town

Point of interest

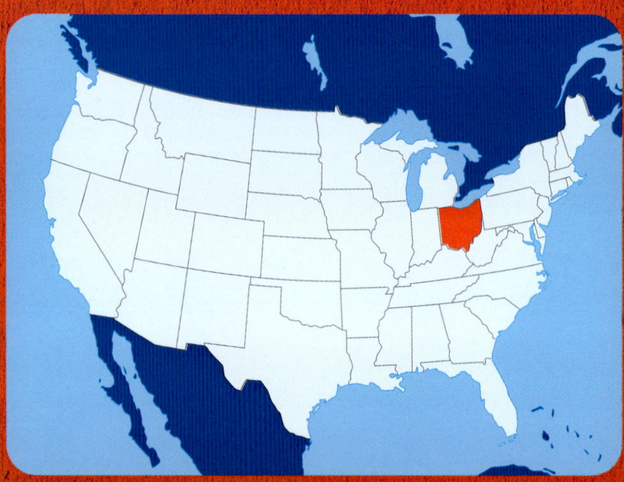

Cleveland

Cedar Point

Columbus

Ohio: The Buckeye State

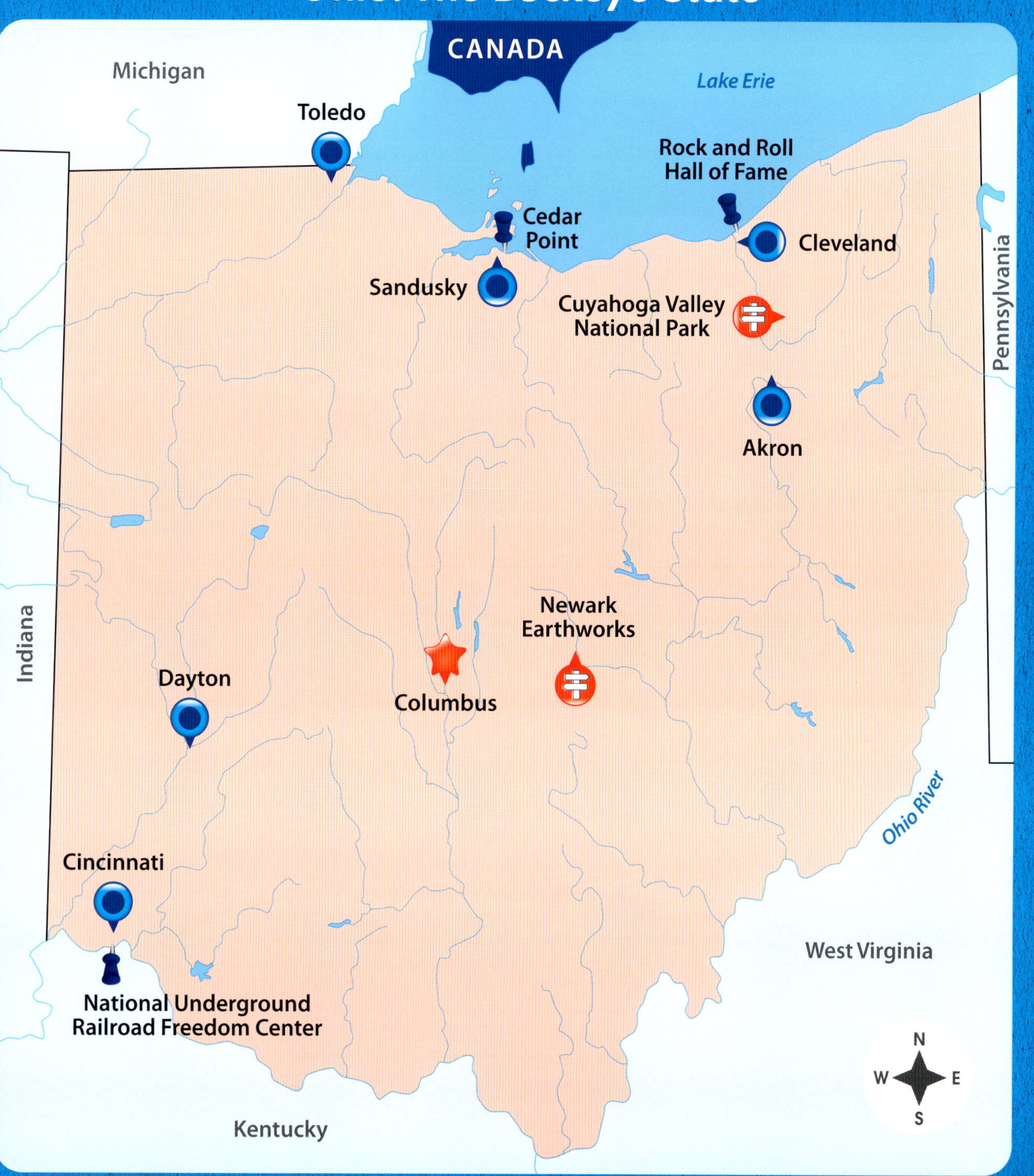

Glossary

ancestors
the people from whom a person is descended and who lived many generations ago

canal
a human-made waterway that allows ships to pass between bodies of water

humid
describing air that has a lot of moisture

manufacturing
the process of making goods to sell

natural resources
materials found in nature that can be used by people

populated
settled or lived in

settled
moved into a new area

Online Resources

To learn more about Ohio, visit our free resource websites below.

Visit **abdocorelibrary.com** or scan this QR code for free Common Core resources for teachers and students, including vetted activities, multimedia, and booklinks, for deeper subject comprehension.

Visit **abdobooklinks.com** or scan this QR code for free additional online weblinks for further learning. These links are routinely monitored and updated to provide the most current information available.

Learn More

Hewson, Anthony K. *Cincinnati Reds.* Abdo, 2023.

Kavon, Kana. *The 50 States.* DK, 2021.

Murray, Julie. *Ohio.* Abdo, 2020.

Index

About the Author

Liz Sonneborn is the author of more than 100 books for young readers. She specializes in American history, world history, biography, American Indian studies, and women's history. Now a resident of Brooklyn, New York, Sonneborn went to elementary school in Newark, Ohio, where she frequently visited the Newark Earthworks.